AMISH
Country
Cooking

AMISH
Country
Cooking

Judith Ferguson

Amish Photography by Jerry Irwin

CRESCENT BOOKS
NEW YORK • AVENEL, NEW JERSEY

RECIPES COMPILED BY JUDITH FERGUSON

EDITED BY JILLIAN STEWART

AMISH PHOTOGRAPHY BY JERRY IRWIN

FOOD PHOTOGRAPHY BY PETER BARRY

RECIPES STYLED BY HELEN BURDETT

DESIGNED BY STONECASTLE GRAPHICS LTD.

CLB 2813
© 1992 Colour Library Books Ltd., Godalming, Surrey, England
All rights reserved
This 1993 edition published by Crescent Books,
distributed by Outlet Book Company, Inc.,
a Random House Company
40 Engelhard Avenue, Avenel, New Jersey 07001
Printed and bound in Singapore
ISBN 0 517 06597 5
8 7 6 5 4 3 2

Contents

INTRODUCTION

Sometimes, there is nothing nicer than plain home cooking – comforting food, rich in tradition, not in sauces and spices. Honest, down-to-earth cooking is just what Amish food is all about.

Some of the first settlers who arrived in eastern Pennsylvania during the early years of the eighteenth century were farmers. They were also strict and devoutly religious, dedicated to cultivating the land and to a simple way of life. They called themselves the Amish after their leader, Bishop Jacob Ammann. In their native Europe, these people were divided from others in their communities by their religious beliefs, and to escape the intolerance and persecution in their homeland, they came to America.

Despite the fact that the English settlers already here christened them Pennsylvania Dutch, the Amish came mostly from Germany. No doubt, "Dutch" was the Americanization of Deutsch, the German name for the country's language and its people.

The Amish have always been a modest, honest, harmonious people, who still live their lives much the same way as they have for centuries, despite the march of time and progress. There is no electricity in the typical Amish community. Lighting comes from gas lamps. Stoves and refrigerators use bottled gas, and central heating comes courtesy of wood-burning stoves or open fireplaces. The horse and buggy provides transportation, and plows are still horse-drawn.

The kitchen is the heart of the home, which is not surprising, as it is very often the warmest room, too! It is the room where the whole family meets first thing in the morning, for dinner, which is the mid-day meal, and in the evening for supper, and of course for companionship.

Amish meals are wholesome and satisfying. The recipes reveal their German origins, but the food still harks back to simpler times in America, as well. Food is plentiful, but not extravagant in preparation. There is certainly enough, but the quantity is never excessive. While grains, wheat, barley, rye and corn are major crops on Amish farms, a certain portion of the land is always reserved for growing fruit and vegetables for use in the kitchen, because part of the Amish tradition is self-sufficiency.

In the typical Amish day, the women set aside time for baking. Bread

making begins even before the laundry commences. The dough is left to rise, then is shaped into loaves or rolls and goes into the oven to bake once the clothes are hung out to dry. A lot of cooking and baking still goes on in old stone ovens out behind the farmhouses. These ovens were built wide enough to hold a large log. Once the fire burned low, the embers were raked over until red hot, and the food would be set to cook. While the recipes are perfectly adaptable to conventional indoor ovens, that characteristic wood-smoked flavor is something that cannot be recaptured inside.

Breakfast is hearty, because there is plenty of work to be done during the day. Dinner could be a filling and warming stew, served with either fresh or canned vegetables, depending on the season. Canning is a major aspect of Amish cooking, too. Nothing is left to go to waste. All the produce of the garden is used in season, and the rest is put up to be eaten and enjoyed all winter long. Pickles, preserves and relishes are all favorite ways to keep the goodness of summer. After dinner, the women might bake cakes, pies or cookies in addition to helping with planting or milking. Supper is an important meal of the day, when everyone is bound to be at home and something special is always on the boil, baking or roasting in the oven.

If you lived in an Amish community, you wouldn't dream of going to a supermarket to buy corned beef. You would make it yourself. What's more, you would probably make about 20 pounds of it! Sausage making would be the same. You and your neighbors might cure 100 pounds of ham at a time, or dry 100 pounds of beef, all to be used throughout the year, because the buggy journey from farm to nearest town can be a very long one indeed.

When the Amish came to this country, they brought with them their favorite recipes. These were traditional, and in spirit they survive to this day. But like other settlers who came to call the United States home, the Amish had to adapt their recipes to what was available in the new land, and so while the recipes speak German, they do so with an American accent. That's just as it should be, because however different they may appear, the Amish people are part of our national history, and our culinary one, as well.

SOUPS & APPETIZERS

Favorite Supper Soup

INGREDIENTS
1lb soup beans
1lb ham slice (bone in)
1 onion, chopped
1lb can plum tomatoes, drained
2 potatoes, peeled and diced
1 tsp dried thyme
1 tsp chopped parsley
Salt and pepper

Soak the beans overnight in cold water. Drain and cover with fresh water. Add the ham slice and bring to the boil in a large pan. Simmer until beans are tender, but not falling apart. Remove the ham and dice it. Discard the bone. Skim any fat from the surface of the beans.

Return the ham to the beans and add the remaining ingredients. Simmer gently until the potatoes are soft. Serve at once with bread or rolls.

*An old barn in the Lonewango Valley,
New York, lies with all its doors ajar to
let in the fresh, early morning air.*

Selling their produce at local markets is a profitable venture for many Amish families.

16

German-Style Vegetable Soup

INGREDIENTS
1lb beef bones
2 tbsps oil
1 whole onion stuck with 1 clove
2 sticks celery, roughly chopped
1 bay leaf
1 carrot, diced
2 cups corn kernels
2 cups shredded cabbage
1 large turnip, peeled and diced
2 cups lima beans
1 tsp flour
½ cup milk
Salt and pepper
3 tbsps chopped parsley
2 cups chopped tomatoes

Brown the beef bones in the oil in a large stock pot. Add the onion, celery and bay leaf and pour over enough water to cover by about 3 inches. Bring to the boil, skimming off any scum that floats to the surface. Simmer for about 2 hours. Strain and discard the bones, vegetables and bay leaf.

Combine the stock with the carrot, corn, cabbage, turnip and beans. Blend the flour and milk together until smooth and mix into the soup. Bring back to the boil, then simmer for 45 minutes. Add salt and pepper to taste and stir in the parsley and tomatoes. Cook a further 15 minutes, or until tomatoes are tender. Serve hot.

Serves 6

Turkey Chowder

INGREDIENTS
Turkey bones
1 bay leaf
3 black peppercorns
1 blade of mace
1 onion, unpeeled
1 cup barley, rinsed
3 stalks celery, sliced
3 carrots, diced
1 cup cut green beans
1 cup corn kernels
2 tbsps chopped parsley

Use the carcass from a roast turkey and dice any leftover meat. Place the carcass in a large pot with the bay leaf, peppercorns, mace and onion. Pour in enough cold water to cover the bones, and cover the pot. Bring to the boil, then simmer, partially covered, for about 2 hours. Strain and reserve the stock. Remove and reserve any meat from the bones.

Combine strained stock, barley, celery, carrots and green beans. Partially cover and bring to the boil. Cook about 1 hour, or until barley is tender. Add the corn after about 30 minutes cooking time. Stir in the chopped parsley and any diced turkey.

Right: two Amish brothers take a welcome break from their chores.

The setting sun brings an orange glow to the regimented rows of hay drying on an Amish farm.

Egg Ball Soup

Ingredients
3lb chicken
1 small onion, unpeeled
1 bay leaf
1 sprig of parsley
1 carrot, sliced
1 stick celery, sliced

EGG BALLS
1 cup flour
½ tsp salt
2 tbsps butter
1 tsp chopped parsley
4 small eggs, beaten
½ cup milk
Parsley to garnish

Place chicken, onion, bay leaf, parsley sprig, carrot and celery in a large pot. Add about 3 quarts of cold water. Cover and bring to the boil. Half cover and simmer for about 2 hours, or until chicken is tender and completely cooked. Remove chicken and use for other recipes. Remove and discard onion, bay leaf and sprig of parsley. Keep the carrot and celery.

To make the egg balls, combine the flour and salt and rub in the butter until the mixture looks like fine breadcrumbs. Stir in the parsley. Mix in the eggs and just enough milk to make a batter thick enough to drop from a spoon.

Bring the soup back to the boil. Lower the heat to simmering and drop in the egg ball mixture by spoonfuls. Cook about 10 minutes, or until the egg balls are firm and rise to the surface. Serve immediately, garnished with parsley.

Serves 6

Split Pea Soup

INGREDIENTS
2 cups split peas
1 ham bone
1 small onion, finely chopped
1 bay leaf
3 tbsps margarine
3 tbsps flour
Salt and pepper
2 cups milk
Chopped fresh mint (optional)
Croutons

Soak the peas overnight in enough water to cover. Place in 3 pints of cold water along with the ham bone, onion and bay leaf. Bring to the boil, then simmer until peas are very tender. Remove the ham bone and scrape off any meat. Remove the bay leaf and purée the soup, if desired, and return the meat to the soup.

Melt margarine and stir in the flour until smooth and well blended. Add salt and pepper and stir in the milk gradually. Cook, stirring constantly until thickened. Add the split pea mixture and cook until very thick. Add the chopped mint, if using. If desired, other chopped herbs may also be used. Serve with croutons and extra mint.

Serves 4-6

At harvest time Amish girls (right) help in the fields as well as doing their normal household duties.

Rich Brown Soup

INGREDIENTS

4 tbsps butter or margarine
10 tbsps flour
3 cups water
2 cups beef bouillon
Salt and pepper
Dash of Worcestershire sauce
Grated cheese
Fresh parsley to garnish

Heat the butter or margarine in a large pot until melted. Stir in the flour, then cook over low heat, stirring constantly, until flour is a rich brown color.

Gradually stir in the water and bouillon. Stir constantly while adding the liquid to prevent lumps from forming. Add salt and pepper and Worcestershire sauce. Cover the pot and simmer slowly about 2 hours to fully develop the flavor. Serve sprinkled with grated cheese and garnished with parsley.

Serves 4

The enduring practicality of horse and buggy (left) helps to make it the preferred mode of transport for the Amish.

25

Deviled Crabs

INGREDIENTS
6 boiled crabs
1 tbsp margarine
2 tbsps flour
1 cup cream
2 tsps dry mustard
1 tsp Worcestershire sauce
Salt and pepper
4 hard-cooked eggs
Dry breadcrumbs
Melted margarine
Chopped parsley

Break of all the crab claws. Crack the large claws and legs and pick out the meat. Reserve the smaller legs. Break crab meat into pieces and discard any cartilage and shell. Separate the bodies from the large shells. Discard the spongy "fingers" and the stomach which is found just under the head. Pick out all the meat and combine it with the claw meat. Clean the upper shells thoroughly.

Melt the margarine and add the flour, stirring well. Stir in the cream, mustard and Worcestershire sauce. Cook over moderate heat, stirring constantly, until thickened. Add salt and pepper to taste. Chop the hard-cooked eggs and add to the sauce with the crab meat. Spoon into the clean crab shells, sprinkle lightly with breadcrumbs and drizzle with melted margarine.

Bake in a preheated 350°F oven for about 10 minutes, or until golden brown. Sprinkle with chopped parsley and serve surrounded by the reserved crab legs.

Serves 6

26

An Amish boy takes the opportunity for a ride home as the hay is gathered.

The farm is quieter in the winter months when time is taken up with tasks such as fixing harnesses and machinery.

Baked Stuffed Tomatoes

INGREDIENTS
6 large tomatoes
2 tbsps butter, melted
2 tbsps finely chopped chives
1 tbsp finely chopped parsley
¼ tsp thyme
¼ tsp sage
2 cups breadcrumbs
½ cup finely grated cheese

Remove the tomato stems and cut out the cores. Cut out the centers and scoop out the insides. Discard seeds, chop pulp and mix with the remaining ingredients, reserving the cheese.

Fill the tomato shells with the stuffing ingredients. Place tomatoes in a baking dish and sprinkle with cheese. Bake in a preheated 350°F oven for about 20-30 minutes, depending on the ripeness of the tomatoes. Serve hot.

Serves 6

Eggs Goldenrod

INGREDIENTS
1 tbsp butter
1 tbsp flour
1 cup milk
Salt and white pepper
4 hard-cooked eggs
Toast
Paprika

Melt the butter in a small saucepan. Remove from the heat and add the flour. Stir in the milk and bring to the boil, stirring constantly, until the sauce thickens. Add salt and pepper to taste.

Chop the egg whites and add them to the sauce. Spoon over hot toast on serving plates. Push the egg yolks though a sieve over the top of the sauce. Sprinkle lightly with paprika and serve immediately.

Serves 4

Right: a horse and buggy pointing its way towards home, silhouetted against the setting sun.

Savory Foldovers

INGREDIENTS
2 cups flour
½ lb butter or margarine
½ lb cream cheese
2oz of liver sausage or finely chopped ham
½ tsp chopped dill
2 tsps Worcestershire sauce
Poppy seeds
Paprika

Sift the flour into a bowl and rub in the butter or margarine until mixture resembles breadcrumbs. Work in the cream cheese and chill overnight.

Mix the liver sausage or ham with the dill and Worcestershire sauce. If desired, use half quantity ham and half liver sausage, adding half the dill and Worcestershire sauce to each for two different fillings.

Preheat the oven to 400°F. Lightly grease several baking sheets. Divide dough into an even number of pieces. The foldovers can be small or large. Roll out each piece on a well-floured surface and cut out a circle with a cookie cutter.

Spread each circle with filling and fold over to make half circles. Sprinkle with poppy seeds and paprika, one for each different filling, if desired. Place on baking sheets and bake until browned – about 15 minutes. The foldovers may be shaped in advance and kept chilled until ready to bake. Serve hot or cold.

Makes about 28

A young Amish boy (left) looks forward to supper after a tiring day helping with the harvest.

Corn Oysters

INGREDIENTS

2 cups corn kernels
2 tbsps flour
¼ tsp salt
Pinch of pepper and sugar
2 eggs, separated
Butter or oil for frying
4 green onions, finely chopped
Fresh parsley to garnish

Mash the corn to break it up slightly, but do not purée it. Mix in the flour, salt, pepper and sugar.

Beat the egg yolks until thick and lemon colored and combine with the corn. Beat the egg white until stiff peaks form and fold into the corn mixture.

Heat a small amount of butter or oil in a frying pan and when hot, drop in the corn mixture by tablespoonfuls. Cook until risen and brown on both sides, turning once. Serve sprinkled with chopped green onions, garnish with sprigs of parsley and accompany with pepper relish.

Serves 4

Some Amish families (right) still harvest their corn crop almost entirely by hand.

An Amish boy makes his way to school through the early morning mist.

Spiced Meat Pots

INGREDIENTS

2 cups cooked beef, pork or veal
2½ cups bouillon
¼ tsp cinnamon
¼ tsp nutmeg
¼ tsp ginger
1½ tbsps thyme
1 tbsp Worcestershire sauce
Salt and pepper
Pinch of cayenne pepper
1 tbsp chopped parsley
2 hard-cooked eggs, chopped
1lb butter
Small bay leaves

Cook the meat and the bouillon until meat is very soft. Mash with a fork and beat in the spices, thyme, Worcestershire sauce, salt, pepper and cayenne pepper.

Fold in the parsley and the hard-cooked eggs, being careful not to break up the eggs. Spoon the mixture into small custard cups and chill.

Melt the butter, then turn up the heat until butter boils, but does not brown. Watch it carefully. Remove from the heat and set aside until the butter fats sink to the bottom and the oil rises to the top. Some salt will float on the surface, but skim that off, then slowly pour off the clearer oil, leaving the milky fat sediments behind. Add these to cooked vegetables, if desired.

Spoon a layer of clarified butter over the surface of the potted meats. Chill until set. Garnish with bay leaves, then add more butter to completely cover the meat. Chill until ready to serve. Serve with toast or rolls. If the butter layer is unbroken, the potted meats will keep fresh for several days.

Serves 4

Beets and Eggs

INGREDIENTS
6 to 16 whole beets (depending on size), peeled
½ cup cider vinegar
½ cup cold water
¼ cup sugar
1 bay leaf
3 allspice berries
Small piece of stick cinnamon
6 hard-cooked eggs
Lettuce
Sour cream
Dill

Place the whole beets in a deep saucepan. Mix the vinegar, cold water and sugar together. Add the bay leaf, allspice berries and cinnamon and pour over the beets.

Cover the pan and bring slowly to the boil. Cook rapidly about 10 minutes then remove from the heat. Let the beets stand in the liquid for several days. Remove the beets and store them in an airtight container in a cool place.

Peel the hard-cooked eggs and add to the beet liquid. Let the eggs pickle for about 2 days in a cool place. To serve, slice or cube the beets. Cut the eggs in halves or quarters and arrange on lettuce leaves. Add a spoonful of sour cream and sprinkle with dill. Serve with rye bread and butter.

Serves 6

Amish farmhouses are large and often have additional apartments built on for the grandparents.

MAIN DISHES

Chicken Pot Pie

INGREDIENTS
4 tbsps margarine
½ onion, chopped
4 tbsps flour
2 cups chicken bouillon
3lbs chicken, cooked, boned and cut into chunks
1 cup cooked, diced potatoes
½ cup corn kernels
½ cup cooked, diced carrot
½ cup peas, blanched
½ cup cut green beans, blanched
1 tbsp chopped parsley
⅓ tsp rubbed sage

TOPPING
1½ cups flour
1 tsp baking powder
¼ tsp salt
½ cup soured cream

Heat the margarine in a saucepan and add the onion. Cook slowly until softened. Add the flour and cook to a pale golden color. Stir in the bouillon and bring to the boil. Cook until thickened, stirring constantly. Combine with the chicken and vegetables. Add the parsley and sage, and spoon into a deep pie plate or a casserole dish.

Preheat the oven to 400°F. Combine flour, baking powder and salt. Gradually work in the sour cream. Press out on a floured surface with your hands; do not roll. Cut into rounds with a biscuit cutter. Place on top of the chicken mixture. Bake 20 minutes, or until the chicken is hot and the topping has risen and browned. Serve immediately.

Serves 4-6

Children (right) are introduced to the work ethic at an early age and quickly learn to enjoy doing their chores.

Fried Chicken with Gravy

INGREDIENTS
3-4 lb chicken
Flour
Pinch of rubbed sage, ground thyme and paprika
Salt and pepper
Milk
Oil
1 cup milk or half and half
Watercress or parsley to garnish

Cut the chicken into 6 pieces, breasts with wings attached, thighs and drumsticks. If desired, cut the back into 2 pieces.

Mix together about 1 cup of flour with a good pinch of the herbs, paprika, salt and pepper. Dip the chicken in milk then coat in flour, shaking off the excess. Reserve 1 tablespoon of the flour.

Heat enough oil in a large frying pan to come at least halfway up the sides of the chicken pieces. When hot, add the chicken, bone-side down first. Fry the chicken over moderate heat until golden brown. Turn over and fry the other side. Lower the heat and cook slowly, with oil barely bubbling, until chicken is tender and cooked through. Turn once or twice to ensure even cooking. Drain cooked chicken on paper towels.

Remove all but 2 tablespoons of the oil from the pan, add the reserved flour and cook until a pale gold color. Gradually whisk in the milk or half and half. Bring to the boil and cook until thickened. Serve the chicken garnished with watercress or parsley. Accompany with mashed potatoes, vegetables and the country gravy.

Serves 4-6

Left: after a hard day's work, the family gathers in the farmhouse to chat or do minor chores such as homework.

Home Barbecued Chicken

INGREDIENTS
½ cup tomato ketchup
3 tbsps vinegar
3 tbsps brown sugar
2 tsps Worcestershire sauce
½ tsp onion salt
¼ tsp garlic powder
⅓ cup oil
4 broiler chicken halves

Combine ketchup, vinegar, brown sugar, Worcestershire sauce, onion salt, garlic powder and oil. Heat gently until just boiling. Cool completely.

Oil the broiler pan and rack and preheat the broiler. Brush the chicken skin with oil and broil about 5 inches away from the heat until skin begins to crisp. Turn the chicken over and broil again until beginning to brown. Turn chicken over again, lower the heat and baste with the sauce several times until the chicken is cooked – about 20 minutes.

Serve the chicken with any remaining sauce. Cucumber Cream Salad makes a good accompaniment.

Serves 8

*Winter snows provide the perfect
opportunity for a sleigh ride.*

Preparing the soil for spring planting requires the strength of a large team of mules.

Country-Style Roast Turkey

INGREDIENTS

3 tbsps butter, melted
8oz sausage meat
1 small onion, chopped finely
2 celery stalks, chopped
4 cups cubed bread, dried
1 tsp salt
Pinch of black pepper
¼ tsp poultry seasoning
1 tbsp chopped parsley
1 egg, beaten
10-12lb turkey
½ cup shortening
½ cup flour

Heat butter in a pan and add the sausage. Cook slowly, breaking up the meat with a fork. When the meat is nearly cooked, add the onion and celery and cook until the meat is done.

Meanwhile, soak the bread in bouillon or water until starting to soften. Combine bread with the sausage mixture and the salt, pepper, poultry seasoning, parsley and egg. Preheat the oven to 450°F.

Remove giblets from the turkey and rinse out the cavity. Fill with the stuffing and put any remaining mixture under the flap of skin at the neck end. Truss or place foil over the opening to keep the stuffing moist.

Mix the shortening and flour and rub the legs, breast, and wings. Place turkey in a roasting pan and cover with a tight fitting lid. Roast for 15 minutes.

Reduce the heat to 400°F and roast for 3½ hours, or until tender and juices run clean. Uncover during the last half of the roasting time.

Make a gravy as in the recipe for Fried Chicken with Gravy, using some of the turkey fat and the pan juices. Carve the turkey and serve it with the gravy, mashed potatoes or sweet potatoes, and vegetables.

Serves 8-10

Salmon Loaf

INGREDIENTS
1lb can of salmon
1 cup cracker crumbs
½ cup milk
1 tbsp butter, melted
2 eggs, beaten
Salt and pepper
Parsley to garnish

Preheat oven to 350°F. Grease a bread pan well. Mix the salmon, cracker crumbs, milk, butter, beaten egg and a pinch of salt and pepper.

Spoon mixture into the pan and smooth the top. Cover with buttered foil and bake in the oven about 30 minutes. Uncover the pan after about 15 minutes to allow the top to brown. Garnish with parsley and serve hot. Delicious with cucumbers in sour cream.

Serves 4

Under the supervision of their parents, Amish children will help with chores such as planting from an early age.

Baked Mackerel

INGREDIENTS
4 mackerel, cleaned
4 tbsps butter
Juice of 1 lemon
MUSTARD SAUCE
1 tbsp butter
1 tbsp flour
1 cup milk
¼ tsp salt
Pinch of white pepper
1 tbsp German style mustard

Preheat the oven to 400°F. Cut the heads off the fish, if desired, and place fish in a baking dish. Dot with butter and sprinkle with lemon juice. Place in the oven and bake about 15 to 20 minutes, depending on the size of the fish.

Meanwhile, melt the butter for the sauce and stir in the flour. Beat in the milk, salt and pepper and cook over moderate heat, stirring constantly, until thickened. Beat in the mustard.

Serve the fish with some of the sauce spooned over and serve the rest of the sauce separately.

Serves 4

A mule team waits patiently while the last of the hay crop is gathered.

Paprika Schnitzel

INGREDIENTS
4 veal cutlets or pork steaks
Flour
Salt and pepper
2 tbsps oil
1 small onion, finely chopped
1 red pepper, de-seeded and sliced
1 tsp paprika
1 cup tomato sauce
1 cup sour cream

Pound the veal or pork between sheets of waxed paper until meat is very thin. Mix flour with a good pinch of salt and pepper and coat the meat, shaking off the excess.

Heat the oil in a large frying pan and when hot place in the meat. Fry on both sides until golden brown, about 5 minutes each side. Remove to a plate and keep them warm.

Add the onion and pepper to the pan and cook slowly until softened but not browned, about 5 minutes. Stir in the paprika and cook 1 minute. Add the tomato sauce and return the cutlets to the pan. Cover and simmer about 20 minutes, or until the meat is tender.

Remove meat and vegetables to a serving dish. Stir sour cream into the pan and cook gently to heat through. Do not let the sour cream boil. Spoon over the meat and serve with dumplings, potatoes or noodles.

Sauerbraten

<u>INGREDIENTS</u>
4lb piece of round or chuck steak
2 cups cider vinegar
2 bay leaves
1 tsp thyme
½ tsp black pepper
6 whole cloves
½ tsp salt
½ cup flour
1 tsp ground allspice
4 tbsps oil
4 carrots, quartered
4 small onions, quartered
4 parsnips or turnips, quartered
12 gingersnaps, crushed finely
1 tbsp brown sugar
Fresh parsley to garnish

Place the meat in a large bowl. Mix the vinegar, bay leaves, thyme, pepper and cloves, and pour over the meat. Add enough water to cover meat completely. Keep in the refrigerator for two days. Drain the meat and reserve the vinegar mixture.

Pat the meat dry with paper towels. Mix together the salt, flour and allspice and rub into the surface of the meat on all sides. Heat oil in a large pot or deep frying pan. When hot, brown the meat well on all sides.

Remove the meat and add the carrots, onions and parsnips or turnips, brown lightly and return the meat to the pan. Pour over 2 cups of the vinegar mixture. Cover the pan and cook over low heat for about 2 hours.

When the meat is tender, remove it to a serving dish along with the vegetables. Skim any fat from the surface of the cooking liquid and stir in the sugar and the crushed gingersnaps. Cook about 10 minutes and spoon some of the sauce over the meat. Serve the rest separately and accompany with boiled or mashed potatoes. Garnish with fresh parsley.

Serves 6-8

54

Right: a group of Amish school-children make their way home under a canopy of colorful fall trees.

Hamburger Roast

INGREDIENTS
3 eggs
2 large potatoes
3lbs lean ground beef
1 onion, chopped finely
Salt and pepper
1 tsp chopped parsley
2 slices of bread, made into crumbs
1 tsp Worcestershire sauce
Flour
¼ lb sliced bacon
Fresh parsley to garnish

Hard-cook the eggs, shell them and keep them in cold water. Peel the potatoes and cut them into chunks. Boil until tender, then mash them and leave to cool.

Combine the mashed potatoes with the ground beef, onion, salt and pepper to taste, parsley, breadcrumbs and Worcestershire sauce.

Divide the meat mixture in half and shape each half into a thick rectangle. Drain the hard-cooked eggs, pat dry and dust lightly with flour. Place the eggs down the center of one of the meat rectangles. Place the other on top and mold meat around the eggs to cover them completely.

Preheat oven to 400°F. Wrap the slices of bacon around the hamburger roast to cover and tie them on with string. Place in a roasting pan and bake for about 1½ hours, or until the meat is completely cooked. Serve hot or cold, garnished with fresh parsley.

Serves 6-8

Left: a retired farmer uses his woodworking skills making chairs to sell in his small shop.

Beef Stew

INGREDIENTS
2½ lbs chuck or round steak
3 tbsps oil
2 onions
2 small turnips, diced
3 carrots, diced
3 potatoes, diced
2 celery stalks, sliced
½ cup flour
½ tsp salt
¼ tsp black pepper
4 cups water
1 bay leaf
1 cup peas

Cut meat into 2-inch pieces, trimming off the fat. Heat the oil in a large pot and fry the meat in small batches until well browned. Remove and set aside. Add the onion, turnips, carrots, potatoes and celery to the pot and cook slowly to brown lightly. Remove and set aside with the meat.

If necessary, add more oil to the pot. Add the flour and cook slowly until a good, rich brown color. Return the meat and vegetables to the pan and add the salt, pepper, water and bay leaf. Bring to the boil, then reduce the heat and simmer the stew about 2 hours or until the meat and vegetables are tender.

Remove the bay leaf and add the peas to the stew. Cook about 15 minutes, or until peas are tender. Serve with potato dumplings, noodles or mashed potatoes.

Serves 4-6

An early morning mist hangs over an Amish farm where the day's work will already have begun.

Roast Pork

INGREDIENTS
6lb pork loin roast
Salt and pepper
1 tsp ground ginger
Flour
2 onions, sliced

*Place pork in a roasting pan and season well
with salt and pepper. Rub over the ground ginger
and dust with flour.*

*Preheat oven to 400°F. Cook the meat at this
temperature until brown on the surface. Lower
the temperature to 350°F and add the onions and
1 cup of water to the pan. Cook about 25 minutes
to the pound at the lower temperature, basting
every 15 minutes.*

*When the pork is cooked through, remove it to
a carving dish and leave it to stand 15 minutes.
Skim all but 1 tablespoon of the fat from the pan
and leave the meat juices and browned onions.
Add 2 tablespoons of flour to the pan and pour in
1½ cups water. Cook slowly until the gravy boils
and thickens, stirring constantly. Carve the meat
and serve with the gravy, potato dumplings and
vegetables.*

Serves 6-8

Cabbage Rolls

INGREDIENTS
2 tbsps oil
1 onion, finely chopped
1 can condensed tomato soup
1 tbsp vinegar
1 tsp sugar
1 tbsp chopped parsley
2 tsps chopped dill
Six large cabbage leaves
½ lb ground pork
½ lb ground beef
⅓ cup uncooked rice
2 celery stalks, chopped
Salt and pepper
1 egg, beaten
Fresh dill to garnish

Heat the oil in a saucepan and add the onion. Cook slowly until softened. Stir in the tomato soup and half a can of water. Add the vinegar, sugar, parsley and dill. Bring to the boil, then simmer about 10 minutes. If very thick, add more water. Set aside.

If the cabbage leaves have thick spines, pare them down slightly to make them easier to roll. Blanch the leaves a few minutes in boiling water to soften them slightly. Drain and pat dry.

Combine the ground meats with the rice, celery, salt and pepper and egg, mixing well.

Put 2 tablespoons of the meat mixture into each cabbage leaf and roll up, tucking in the sides. Secure each roll with a toothpick. Place the rolls in a saucepan. Season the sauce to taste and pour it over the rolls. Cover the pan and place over low heat.

Cook slowly until the meat is done and the rice is cooked tender – at least 2 hours. Serve immediately, garnished with fresh dill.

Serves 4-6

60

Courting couples enjoy the day of rest.
Going "steady" generally results in
marriage for the Amish.

Traditional dress is worn by young Amish women attending church.

Kraut and Chops

INGREDIENTS
2lb can of sauerkraut
3 tbsps oil
8 pork chops
2 apples, cored and sliced
2 tbsps brown sugar
3 tbsps caraway seeds

Drain the sauerkraut well and rinse in cold water. Leave to dry.

Heat the oil in a large frying pan and brown the chops slowly on both sides. Remove and keep them warm.

Combine the sauerkraut with the apples, brown sugar and caraway seeds. Add to the pan and cook slowly until the pan juices have been absorbed. Add about 1½ cups water and return the chops to the pan. Cover the pan and cook slowly until the chops are done and the water has evaporated. Watch the sauerkraut carefully and add more water if necessary during cooking to prevent burning.

Serves 4-8

Glazed Ham

INGREDIENTS
10lb ham
Whole cloves
1 cup brown sugar
1 tbsp dry mustard
1½ tbsps flour
Canned pineapple slices

Place ham in a pot and cover with water. Bring slowly to the boil, then simmer for 1 hour. Allow to cool in the water, then remove ham and pour off water. Using a sharp knife, remove the rind from the ham. Omit these steps when using precooked ham.

Preheat oven to 325°F. Score the fat at 1-inch intervals and stick with cloves. Combine the brown sugar, dry mustard and flour and press on all sides about 1½ inches thick. Pour the juice from the pineapple over the top of the ham. Place on the pineapple slices.

Bake about 25 minutes to the pound, basting often. Lower the oven temperature to 300°F about 15 minutes before the end of cooking time. Coat with more brown sugar mixture and bake 15 minutes without basting for a crisp glaze.

Allow the ham to stand for 15 minutes before carving.

Serves 8-10

A young girl intent on enjoying the freshness of a newly harvested melon.

Spicy Roast Lamb

A young Amish girl digs up potatoes for the evening meal.

INGREDIENTS
8 small onions
1 leg of lamb
Salt and pepper
Flour
Pinch of sugar
½ cup hot water
1 tbsp Worcestershire sauce

Preheat oven to 450°F. Peel and parboil the onions.

Wipe the surface of the leg of lamb with a clean, damp cloth. Season with salt and pepper and dust with flour. Place in a roasting pan and cook for 15 minutes. Reduce the temperature to 350°F. Place the onions around the lamb and sprinkle them lightly with sugar. Finish cooking the lamb for 20 minutes per pound.

After 15 minutes cooking at the lower temperature, mix the hot water and Worcestershire sauce and pour over the lamb. Baste every 30 minutes with the mixture, turning the onions at the same time. Add more water, if necessary.

Remove the lamb to a carving dish along with the onions. Remove all but 2 tablespoons of the fat from the roasting pan. Stir in 4 tablespoons flour and cook about 5 minutes. Stir in 2 cups of water and bring to the boil. Simmer, stirring constantly, until thickened. Season to taste and serve with lamb and onions.

Amish Omelet

INGREDIENTS
¼ lb bacon, diced
¼ lb ham, diced
¼ lb mushrooms, sliced
6 green onions, sliced
4 eggs
4 tbsps milk
Salt and pepper

Fry the bacon in a heavy frying pan until crisp. Remove and drain on paper towels. Add the ham and mushrooms to the pan and cook until mushrooms are tender, then return the bacon to the pan and add the onions.

Beat the eggs and the milk with a pinch of salt and pepper. Pour over the mixture in the pan and cook for about 3 minutes, stirring frequently until beginning to set. Allow to cook slowly without stirring until eggs are set. Serve immediately with toast and sliced tomatoes.

Serves 2-4

Left: whilst his brother toils with the plow the youngest boy enjoys guiding the mule.

Smoked Sausage with Gravy

INGREDIENTS
1 tbsp margarine
1½ lb smoked sausage
1 onion, sliced
½ lb mushrooms, sliced
1 tbsp flour
1½ cups beef bouillon
Chopped dill

Heat the margarine in a frying pan and when hot add the sausage. Cook slowly, turning frequently until browned.

Remove sausage from the pan and keep it warm. Add the onion to the pan and cook until golden brown. Add the mushrooms and cook until softened. Place with the sausage.

If necessary, add more margarine to the pan. Stir in the flour and cook until lightly browned. Stir in the bouillon and bring to the boil. Cook, stirring constantly, until thickened.

Slice the sausage into serving portions and return it to the pan along with onions and mushrooms to heat through. Sprinkle with chopped dill and serve with sauerkraut or potatoes.

Hay is first cut in June, but is only one of many crops gathered during the year.

VEGETABLE
& SIDE DISHES

Wilted Lettuce

INGREDIENTS
1 head Romaine lettuce, washed
8 strips of bacon
2 tbsps butter
½ cup cream
2 eggs
½ tsp salt
1 tbsp sugar
4 tbsps cider vinegar
Pepper
Paprika

Tear lettuce into large pieces and place in a bowl. Dice the strips of bacon and fry slowly until some of the fat renders. Raise the heat and cook bacon until crisp. Scatter over the lettuce.

Melt the butter in the pan with any remaining bacon fat. Stir in the cream and bring to the boil, then simmer gently. Beat the eggs with the salt, sugar, vinegar and pepper. Pour into the cream mixture and cook until the consistency of thick custard, stirring constantly.

Pour over the lettuce and bacon, and toss to coat. Sprinkle with paprika and serve immediately as a side dish with meat or poultry.

Serves 4

Left: a field is the perfect playground for this child who has the good fortune to grow up in idyllic surroundings.

73

Scalloped Sweet Potatoes

INGREDIENTS
6 even-sized sweet potatoes
4 tbsps butter
½ cup light brown sugar
1 tsp grated nutmeg
Pinch of salt
½ cup chopped walnuts or pecans
1½ cups sliced apples

Place unpeeled sweet potatoes in cold water and boil until tender. Drain and peel while still warm. Cut into slices about ¼ inch thick.

Melt butter and, when foaming, stir in the brown sugar, nutmeg and salt. Cook slowly until the sugar dissolves and forms a syrup.

Place a layer of sweet potato slices in a casserole dish and scatter over some of the chopped nuts. Spoon over some of the syrup, then add a layer of apples. Continue until all the sweet potatoes, nuts, syrup and apples have been used, ending with a layer of apples.

Cover and bake in a preheated 350°F oven for about 50 minutes. Uncover the casserole to allow apples to brown slightly during the last 15 minutes of cooking.

Serves 4

Young children are under the constant supervision of their mothers and are expected to help her wherever possible.

The Amish are divided about the ethics of growing tobacco, but it is a crucial source of income for many families.

Noodle and Vegetable Ring

INGREDIENTS

1 cup egg noodles
Oil
3 tbsps butter or margarine
3 tbsps flour
1½ cups milk
Salt, pepper and paprika
½ lb Cheddar cheese, grated
2 eggs, beaten
½ cup cooked peas and carrots
1 cup cooked broccoli flowerets
½ cup cooked corn kernels
1 pimento cap, diced
Paprika

Cook the egg noodles in about 3 cups of boiling water until just tender. Drain well and toss with a little oil to prevent sticking.

Melt the butter or margarine in a saucepan, then stir in the flour. Cook about 1 minute, then gradually beat in the milk until smooth. Add a good pinch of salt, pepper and paprika. Bring the sauce to the boil, stirring constantly, until thick. Add the cheese and stir until melted. Divide the sauce in two.

Preheat oven to 350°F. Add half the sauce and the eggs to the noodles and mix thoroughly. Spoon the noodle mixture into a well-greased ring mold. Place the mold in a roasting pan containing enough hot water to come halfway up the sides of the mold. Bake for about 45 minutes, or until completely set.

Meanwhile, cook the vegetables and combine them and the diced pimento cap with the remaining cheese sauce. If the sauce is too thick, thin it down with a little more milk. Unmold the noodle ring on a large platter and sprinkle with paprika. Spoon the vegetables in their sauce into the middle.

Serves 4-6

Breaded Eggplant Slices

INGREDIENTS
2 eggplants
Flour
Salt and pepper
2 eggs, beaten
Fine cracker crumbs
Oil for frying

Cut the eggplants into thin slices. Sprinkle with salt and place in a single layer on paper towels. Leave for about 30 minutes or until the salt draws out the juices. Rinse and pat dry.

Mix the flour with a good pinch of salt and pepper. Coat the eggplant slices in the flour, shaking off the excess. Dip the slices in the beaten egg, then coat in the cracker crumbs.

Heat about ½ inch of oil in a large frying pan. When very hot, lower in the eggplant slices carefully. Fry a few minutes on each side, or until crisp and golden brown. Drain on paper towels. Serve with ketchup, if desired.

Children are introduced to the ways of the farm at an early age and soon become familiar with handling crops.

Sauerkraut

INGREDIENTS
2 tbsps oil
1 onion, sliced
1 quart canned sauerkraut, rinsed
1 potato, coarsely grated
1 apple, peeled, cored and sliced
Brown sugar
1 tbsp caraway seed

Heat the oil in a large pot and add the onion. Cook until golden.

Stir in the sauerkraut and cook about 5 minutes. Add the potato and apple, and cover with boiling water. Cook slowly about 30 minutes.

Taste and add brown sugar as desired. Stir in the caraway seeds. Cover the pan and cook very slowly for a further 30 minutes. Serve with duck, pork or sausages.

Renowned for the quality of their fruit and vegetables, many Amish families successfully sell their produce at market.

Cabbage-Stuffed Peppers

INGREDIENTS

6 sweet red peppers
3 tbsps butter or margarine
1 small onion, finely sliced
1 head white or green cabbage, shredded
1 tbsp chopped dill
2 tsps mild mustard
2 tbsps vinegar
2 tbsps sugar
Salt and pepper
Fresh dill to garnish

Cut off the tops of the peppers and remove the seeds and cores. Blanch the peppers and tops in boiling water for about 5 minutes. Remove and drain upside down on paper towels.

Heat the butter or margarine in a large saucepan and add the onion and cabbage. Cook about 10 minutes, stirring frequently. Stir in the chopped dill, mustard, vinegar and sugar. Taste and add more vinegar or sugar as necessary, together with salt and pepper.

Preheat oven to 300°F. Spoon the cabbage filling into the peppers and replace the tops. Place in a tight-fitting baking dish. Pour in a little water and cover the dish with foil. Bake 35 to 45 minutes, or until the peppers are just tender. Garnish with fresh dill and serve hot as an accompaniment to meat.

Serves 6

Creamy Lima Beans

INGREDIENTS
1lb lima beans
4 potatoes, diced
2oz smoked ham
1¼ cups half and half
1 tbsp butter
1 tbsp chopped parsley
Nutmeg

Remove lima beans from their pods, if necessary. Frozen lima beans may also be used. Place the beans and potatoes in cold water, cover and bring slowly to the boil. Simmer, half covered, until tender, about 15 or 20 minutes.

Drain the vegetables and return to the pan. Add the ham and pour in the half and half. Add the butter and heat until almost boiling. Stir in the parsley and sprinkle with nutmeg to serve.

Serves 4

Right: an Amish girl gathers beans, probably to be eaten that very day.

Buggies await their new owners outside an Amish shop in Pennsylvania.

Country Baked Beans

INGREDIENTS
2 cups navy beans
¼ lb salt pork
1 large onion, chopped
2 tbsps molasses
8oz can tomatoes, chopped
1 tsp mustard
1½ tbsps dark brown sugar
½ cup boiling water
Fresh parsley to garnish

Soak the beans overnight in enough cold water to cover. Blanch the pork in boiling water a few minutes to remove some of the salt, then drain. Cut pork into small strips.

Drain the beans and cover with fresh water. Bring to the boil, then simmer until the skins burst. Add the onion, molasses, tomatoes and their juice, mustard, sugar and water to the beans. Place beans in a baking dish, scatter over the pork strips and cover the dish.

Preheat oven to 300°F and bake the beans for about 6 hours, or until completely tender. Uncover during the last hour to brown the pork. Garnish with fresh parsley.

Serves 6

Mashed Butternut Squash

INGREDIENTS
2 butternut squash, peeled
2 tbsps butter
2 tbsps maple syrup
Salt and pepper

Cut the butternut squash in half and scoop out the seeds. Cut into even-sized pieces. Place in a pan with just enough water to cover the squash halfway.

Cover the pan and bring to the boil. Simmer until the squash is very tender. Drain well.

Return the squash to the pan and place over moderate heat. As the squash dries, mash to a purée. Beat in the butter, maple syrup and a pinch of salt and pepper. Mix well. Serve piping hot.

Serves 4-6

Fruits such as cherries are used to make delightful pies and preserves, and any extra will be sold at market.

Potato Dumplings

Amish children patiently wait to take the produce to market with their parents.

INGREDIENTS
10 slices white bread, crusts trimmed
1 onion, grated
2 eggs, beaten
½ tsp finely chopped parsley
½ tsp chopped dill
6 raw potatoes, peeled
Salt and pepper
Pinch of nutmeg

Bring a large pot of water to the boil. Soak the bread in cold water and squeeze out as much as possible. Mix bread with the onion, eggs, parsley and dill.

Grate the potatoes finely and mix into the bread mixture. Add salt and pepper to taste and a pinch of nutmeg.

Shape the mixture into balls with floured hands. Drop dumplings into the boiling water and cook about 15 minutes. When the dumplings are cooked, they will rise to the surface. You may need to turn them several times. Remove from the water and drain on paper towels. Serve with stews.

Serves 6

Potato Salad

INGREDIENTS
10 red potatoes, boiled in their skins
2 stalks of celery, sliced thinly
1 small onion, chopped finely
1 tbsp chopped parsley
3 hard-cooked eggs, sliced
1½ cups mayonnaise
1 tbsp mustard
Pinch of salt and pepper
1 pimento, chopped
2 baby dill pickles, sliced
Paprika
Fresh parsley to garnish

Peel the potatoes while still warm. Dice them and place in a large bowl with the celery, onion, and parsley. Add the hard-cooked eggs, reserving a few slices for the top of the salad.

Mix together the mayonnaise, mustard, salt and pepper. Add pimento and dill pickles to the salad and combine with the mayonnaise, coating the ingredients thoroughly. Place egg slices on top and sprinkle with paprika. Garnish with fresh parsley.

Serves 4-6

Right: Amish children find fun in their daily chores.

Cucumber Cream Salad

INGREDIENTS
1 large cucumber, thinly sliced
Salt
½ cup sour cream
1 tbsp vinegar
Pepper
1 tsp chopped dill
Paprika
Sprigs of dill to garnish

Place cucumber slices in a colander and sprinkle with salt. Leave to drain for several hours. Rinse well in cold water and pat dry. Place in a bowl.

Mix sour cream, vinegar, pepper and dill together and combine with the cucumbers. Sprinkle with paprika and garnish with sprigs of dill, if available.

Serves 4-6

Left: collecting milk – just one of the chores which a housewife may have to do while the men are busy in the fields.

Mustard Pickles

INGREDIENTS
2 cups diced cucumbers
2 cups pearl onions, peeled
2 cups diced green peppers
1 cup salt
2 heads cauliflower, cut into small flowerets
4 cups distilled white vinegar
1 cup flour
1½ cups sugar
1 cup mild mustard
2 tbsps celery seed
1 tbsp turmeric

Place cucumbers, onions and green peppers in a colander and sprinkle with salt. Leave to stand overnight. Rinse and cover with water. Bring to the boil, then simmer until thoroughly cooked. Drain well and, when cold, mix with the cauliflower.

Mix ½ cup of the vinegar with the flour to make a thick paste. Bring remaining vinegar to the boil. Mix the sugar, mustard, celery seed and turmeric into the vinegar and flour paste and whisk into the boiling vinegar. Add the vegetables and cook until beginning to thicken. Remove from the heat and pour into sterilized jars. Seal and store for several weeks before using.

*Canning jars filled with an array of
delicious fruit and vegetables are often
sold at market alongside fresh produce.*

94

A well-stocked larder is the result of many long hours spent preparing and canning produce.

Pepper Relish

INGREDIENTS
5 small onions
8 sweet green peppers
8 sweet red peppers
2 cups white distilled vinegar
¾ cup sugar
1½ tbsps salt
2 tbsps celery seed

Cut the onions into small dice. Cut peppers in half and remove the cores and seeds. Cut into dice the same size as the onions. Place in a large bowl and pour over boiling water. Let stand 5 minutes then drain. Cover with more boiling water and leave to stand 10 minutes. Drain overnight in a colander.

Combine onions and peppers with the vinegar, sugar, salt and celery seeds in a large pot. Bring to the boil, then cook rapidly for about 20 minutes. While still hot, pour into sterilized jars and seal tightly. Store for several weeks before serving.

Pickled Red Cabbage

INGREDIENTS
Red cabbage, shredded
Salt
White distilled vinegar
Sugar
**Pepper, ground nutmeg, cinnamon, allspice and
  celery seed**
Granny Smith apples, cored and sliced (optional)
Fresh parsley to garnish

*Use as many heads of cabbage as you like. Place
shredded cabbage in a large bowl and sprinkle
liberally with salt. Leave overnight. Drain all the
moisture from the cabbage then leave for several
hours at room temperature.*

*Pour enough vinegar over the cabbage to
cover, then strain it off into a pan. Add 1 cup of
sugar for every gallon of vinegar. Add a good
pinch of each of the spices and the celery seed.
Boil for 7 or 8 minutes, then pour over the
cabbage. Spoon into stoneware jars or glass
storage jars and cover. Store in a cool place for
several weeks before using. If desired, add a
sliced apple for every two cups of cabbage just
before serving. Garnish with fresh parsley.*

Serves 4-6

This stall shows the extent of Amish self sufficiency, with quilts, preserves and fresh produce all for sale.

DESSERTS

Cake & Wine Custard Pudding

<u>INGREDIENTS</u>
1 pound cake
4 coconut macaroons
1 cup red or black raspberries
2 nectarines, sliced
1 cup German white wine
1 tbsp cornstarch
1 tbsp lemon juice
3 eggs, separated
¾ cup sugar
Chopped nuts

Break the pound cake and macaroons in 1-inch pieces and place in a baking dish with the fruit.

Heat the wine until just boiling. Mix the cornstarch with the lemon juice and the egg yolks. Beat in some of the hot wine and then add the egg mixture to the rest of the wine. Place over low heat and cook, stirring constantly, until the mixture coats the back of a spoon. Pour over the cake and fruit. Allow to cool completely.

When cold, beat the egg whites until stiff peaks form. Gradually beat in the sugar until the meringue is stiff and glossy. Spoon on top of the pudding and sprinkle with nuts. Bake 5 to 10 minutes in a 425°F oven until pale brown. Serve immediately.

Serves 6-8

Right: the market stall in summer, when the harvests mean there is a plentiful supply of fruits and vegetables.

Fruit Fritters

INGREDIENTS
⅓ cup butter
½ cup sugar
2 eggs, separated
2 cups flour
3 tsps baking powder
½ tsp salt
1 cup milk
½ tsp vanilla extract
½ tsp lemon juice
¾ cup chopped peaches
¾ cup chopped apples
Oil for frying
Powdered sugar
Whipped cream
Nutmeg or cinnamon

Cream the butter and sugar until light. Beat in the egg yolks until light and creamy. Combine the dry ingredients and add gradually along with the milk. Fold in the vanilla and lemon juice. Beat the egg whites until stiff, and fold into the mixture. Divide the mixture in half and add peaches to one half and apples to the other.

Heat oil in a deep pan or deep-fat fryer to 375°F. Drop the batter in by large spoonfuls. When fritters rise to the surface, turn them over to brown all sides. Drain well on paper towels. Sprinkle with powdered sugar. Serve hot, topped with whipped cream sprinkled with nutmeg or cinnamon.

Serves 6

Left: a good crop of strawberries means a delicious dessert for the supper table.

103

Shoo-Fly Pie

INGREDIENTS

PASTRY
1 cup flour
¼ tsp salt
⅓ cup shortening
1 tbsp butter
Milk

CRUMB MIXTURE
¾ cup flour
½ tsp cinnamon
Pinch of nutmeg, ground cloves and ginger
Pinch of salt
½ cup brown sugar
2 tbsps shortening

FILLING
½ tbsp baking soda
¾ cup boiling water
½ cup molasses
1 egg yolk, beaten well

To prepare the pie crust, blend flour, salt, shortening and butter until the mixture resembles breadcrumbs. Mix in enough milk to form a firm dough. Chill about 10 minutes, then roll out and line an 8-inch pie plate.

To make the crumb mixture, combine flour with spices, salt and sugar. Blend in the shortening until the mixture forms coarse crumbs.

To make the filling, dissolve the baking soda in the boiling water and blend in the molasses and egg yolk thoroughly. Preheat oven to 400°F. Fill the pie with alternating layers of the crumb and filling mixture, ending with crumbs. Bake until crust edges start to brown. Lower the temperature to 350°F and bake about 20 minutes, or until filling is set. Serve warm or cold with whipped cream or vanilla ice cream.

Serves 6

As the sign illustrates Shoo-fly Pie is a great favorite with ousiders as well as the Amish.

Dutch Pancake

INGREDIENTS
Butter
½ cup flour
Pinch of salt
3 eggs, beaten
½ cup milk
Powdered sugar
1 lemon

Preheat oven to 400°F. Butter a large, round cake pan. Sift the flour into a bowl along with the salt. Make a well in the center of the flour and add the eggs and milk. Beat with a wooden spoon, gradually mixing in flour from the outside until a smooth batter is formed.

Place the pancake in the oven and bake about 25 minutes, until well risen and golden brown. Serve sprinkled with powdered sugar, with lemon wedges to squeeze over the top.

Left: looking after the milking operation, which is often the responsibility of the women in the family.

Apple Strudel

INGREDIENTS
2 tbsps shortening
2½ cups flour
1 tsp salt
2 eggs, beaten
½ cup warm water
½ cup butter, melted
4 cups peeled, sliced apples
Grated rind and juice of 1 lemon
1 cup brown sugar
½ cup golden raisins
½ cup chopped walnuts
½ cup fine breadcrumbs
½ tsp cinnamon

Rub the shortening into the flour and salt until mixture resembles breadcrumbs. Mix in the eggs and enough water to make a soft, but not sticky, dough.

Knead the dough, then throw or beat it against a clean table top until it is smooth and elastic and stretches easily without tearing.

Cover the table with a clean cloth such as a tablecloth or a pastry cloth, and roll out the dough to a 15-inch square. Using your finger-tips, pull the dough from the middle, out to the ends, lifting it each time, until it is as thin as tissue paper. Reserve 3 tablespoons of the melted butter and sprinkle the rest over the pastry.

Combine all the remaining ingredients and the reserved butter and scatter the mixture evenly over the pastry. Fold in the outer edges and lift one end of the cloth to roll the pastry over the filling to form a long roll about 4 inches thick.

Preheat the oven to 400°F and place the strudel on a baking sheet. If it won't fit, form it into a crescent shape. Bake about 20 minutes, or until golden brown and flaky. Allow to cool until barely warm, then sprinkle with powdered sugar. Cut into serving pieces and serve with ice cream or whipped cream.

A barn raising is a great event for the Amish and one which illustrates their willingness to help one another.

Cheesecake

INGREDIENTS
½ cup shortening
1½ cups flour
¼ tsp salt
Ice water
1lb cream cheese
4 eggs, beaten
1 cup sugar
2 tbsps flour
1 cup cream
1 tsp vanilla extract
Cinnamon

Rub shortening into the flour and salt until the mixture resembles breadcrumbs. Work in enough ice water to make a firm dough. Roll out on a floured surface and use to line the bottom and sides of a 10-inch springform pan.

Preheat the oven to 400°F. Place a sheet of foil over the pastry and cover it with rice or dry beans. Bake the pastry until just starting to brown lightly. Remove the foil and rice or beans and return pastry to the oven for 5 minutes to bake the bottom.

Beat the cream cheese to soften, and gradually beat in the eggs. Beat in the sugar and flour. Stir in the cream gradually and add the vanilla extract. Pour into the pastry shell and place in the oven. Lower the temperature to 325°F and bake for 40 minutes. Sprinkle with cinnamon and cool completely before serving.

Left: horses are essential in the successful running of an Amish farm.

111

Potato Custard Pie

INGREDIENTS
Pastry from the Cheesecake recipe
1 medium-sized potato
2 tbsps butter
¾ cup sugar
2 eggs, separated
1 tsp vanilla extract
⅓ cup milk
½ cup sour cream
Nutmeg

Prepare the pastry and use it to line an 8-inch pie dish. Chill until needed.

Boil the potato whole and unpeeled, which will take at least 30 minutes – do not let it boil too rapidly. Drain and peel the potato while it is still warm. Mash the potato in a pan over heat to evaporate excess water.

Add the butter and sugar to the potato, and allow to cool completely. Preheat the oven to 400°F. Beat in the egg yolk, vanilla extract and milk. Beat the egg whites until stiff but not dry and fold into the potato mixture.

Spoon into the pie shell and bake about 25 minutes, or until the custard is set. Insert a toothpick into the center to test. If it comes out clean, the pie is done. Spread with sour cream and sprinkle with nutmeg. Return to the oven for 5 minutes. Cool completely before serving.

Young Amish boys help to gather in the crops on their father's farm.

112

Fried Fruit Pies

INGREDIENTS
1 cup mixed dried fruit
Brown sugar
2 cups flour
1 tsp salt
½ cup shortening
⅓ cup cold water
Oil for deep frying
Powdered sugar
Sour cream

Place the fruit in water and bring slowly to the boil. Simmer about 10 minutes, then cover the pan and leave until the fruit has softened. Drain, remove any stones from the fruit, and chop coarsely. If necessary, sweeten with a little brown sugar.

Mix together the flour and salt. Rub in the shortening until the mixture looks like breadcrumbs. Work in the cold water to make a firm dough.

Roll out the dough on a floured board and cut into 4-inch circles. Place 1½ tablespoons of the mixture onto each circle and brush the pastry with water. Fold over and seal the edges tightly.

Heat oil in a deep fryer or frying pan to 375°F. Place two or three pies at a time in the hot oil and cook until golden brown on all sides. The pies will rise to the surface when one side is cooked. Turn once or twice until evenly done. Drain on paper towels.

Serve warm, dusted with powdered sugar. Spoon sour cream on top, if desired.

Angel Food Cake

INGREDIENTS

CAKE
11 egg whites
1½ cups granulated sugar
1 cup flour
1 tsp cream of tartar
Pinch of salt
1 tsp vanilla extract

FROSTING
2 cups sugar
8 tbsps cold water
2 egg whites
Raspberries
Mint leaves to decorate

Preheat oven to 250°F. Beat the egg whites until stiff peaks form. Sift all the dry ingredient together several times, then sift again over the egg whites.

Fold the dry ingredients into egg whites along with the vanilla. Spoon mixture into an ungreased angel food pan and bake for about 1 hour, or until cake is well risen and golden brown. The top should spring back when lightly touched.

Turn the pan upside down on its legs. If the pan doesn't have legs, place upside down over the neck of a bottle. Leave until completely cold. The cake should slide easily out of the pan. Remove the tube and place on a wire cooling rack.

To make the frosting, combine the sugar with the water in a pan and boil until the syrup forms a long thread. Beat the egg white until stiff, then gradually beat the hot sugar syrup into it. Mash one or two of the berries and sieve out the seeds. Beat into the frosting to tint it light pink. Spread immediately over the cake, forming peaks and swirls in the frosting with a knife. Serve with the remaining raspberries. If desired, use vanilla or peppermint extract to flavor the icing and tint pink with food coloring. Decorate with extra raspberries and mint leaves.

*Older Amish children will look after
their younger brothers and sisters and
give them guidance with their chores.*

As their horse strides out, an Amish couple huddle together in their buggy for warmth.

Cottage Pudding

INGREDIENTS
½ **cup butter or margarine**
1 cup sugar
1 egg, beaten
2½ cups flour
4 tsps baking powder
¼ tsp salt
1 cup milk
Grated rind of an orange
2 tbsps currants

PUDDING SAUCE
½ **cup sugar**
1 tbsp flour
Juice of 1 orange
Boiling water
2 tbsps butter
1 tbsp lemon juice

Preheat oven to 350°F. Cream the butter or margarine together until light and fluffy. Beat in the egg. Sift the dry ingredients and add them, alternating with the milk, to the creamed butter. Stir in the grated orange rind and the currants. Squeeze the orange juice for the sauce. Pour the pudding mixture into a well greased cake pan and bake for about 35 minutes.

To make the sauce, mix the sugar and flour together in the top part of a double boiler. Pour orange juice into a 1 pint glass measuring cup and add enough boiling water to make 2 cups of liquid. Gradually beat into the sugar and flour. Place the mixture over simmering water and cook until it thickens. Beat in the butter and lemon juice.

To serve, cut warm pudding into squares and pour over the sauce. Leftovers may be served cold.

Lemon Sponge Pie

INGREDIENTS
Pastry (quantity as for Cheesecake recipe)

LEMON SPONGE FILLING
1 cup sugar
2 eggs, separated
Juice and rind of 1 lemon
1 tbsp margarine, melted
3 tbsps flour
1 cup milk
Lemon slices to decorate
Powdered sugar

Prepare the pastry in the same way as for the Cheesecake recipe. Line a 10-inch pie plate. Chill before filling with the sponge mixture. Do not pre-bake the pastry.

Preheat oven to 350°F. Beat the sugar and egg yolks together until thick. Stir in the lemon juice, rind, margarine and flour. Add the milk and mix well.

Beat the egg whites until stiff peaks form, and fold into the lemon mixture. Pour into the pastry and bake the pie for about 50 minutes, or until filling is puffed and set and pastry is golden. Allow to cool, then decorate with lemon slices and sprinkle with powdered sugar. The pie can be served with whipped cream, if desired.

For safety's sake local authorities insist buggies carry warning triangles (right) to enable them to use public roads.

CAKES, COOKIES & BREADS

Sticky Buns

INGREDIENTS
¼ cup warm water
½ yeast cake
1 cup lukewarm milk
½ tsp salt
3 cups flour
Brown sugar
4 tbsps butter, softened
1 tsp cinnamon
½ cup raisins
3 tbsps chopped citron peel
½ cup chopped pecans

Combine water and yeast. Leave to stand until frothy – about 5 minutes. Stir in the milk. Combine salt, flour and 1 teaspoon brown sugar in a large bowl. Make a well in the center of the dry ingredients and pour in the yeast mixture. Mix to a soft dough.

Knead the dough about 10 minutes on a floured surface. When it is smooth and elastic, place the dough in an oiled bowl and cover with a damp towel. Place bowl in a warm place and leave about 2 hours, or until the dough triples in size.

Knock the air out of the dough and knead again a few minutes. Roll out the dough to a rectangle about ¼ inch thick. Spread over the butter and sprinkle with cinnamon, raisins, citron peel and about 1 tablespoon brown sugar. Roll up like a jelly roll and cut into ¾-inch-thick slices. Place close together in a lightly buttered baking pan. Allow to rise again for about 20 minutes. Sprinkle the top liberally with brown sugar and scatter over the pecans. Bake in a pre-heated 400°F oven for about 20 to 25 minutes.

Makes 1 dozen

Some Amish families turn their skills into viable businesses, such as this pretzel bakery in Pennsylvania.

123

Cinnamon Almond Slices

INGREDIENTS
2 eggs
½ cup sugar
2 tbsps ice water
¾ cup flour
1 tsp cinnamon
Pinch of salt
½ tsp baking powder
¾ cup sliced almonds
Granulated sugar

Preheat oven to 350°F. Beat the eggs and sugar together until light and fluffy. Beat in the ice water.

Sift the flour, cinnamon, salt and baking powder into the egg mixture. Add the almonds and mix thoroughly.

Pour batter into a well-greased square cake pan. Sprinkle the top with sugar. Bake about 25 minutes. Allow to cool, then cut into slices.

Makes 8 slices

Left: pets are often kept by Amish children and looking after them is the child's first taste of responsibility.

Oatmeal Cookies

INGREDIENTS
1½ cups Quaker Oats
½ cup sugar
¼ tsp salt
½ tsp baking powder
½ cup currants
¼ cup chopped almonds
1 egg, beaten
½ tsp almond extract
3 tbsps butter, melted

Combine the oats, sugar, salt, baking powder, currants and almonds in a bowl.

Add the egg, combined with the almond extract and the butter. Mix well with the dry ingredients.

Preheat the oven to 350°F and lightly grease several baking sheets. Drop the mixture by teaspoonfuls onto the sheets and bake about 5 minutes. Remove the cookies from the baking sheets while still warm and leave to cool on wire racks.

The morning's milk yield stands at the end of the farm lane awaiting collection by the local dairy.

Grandma's Lemon Poundcake

INGREDIENTS
1lb sugar
1lb butter
10 eggs
1lb flour
½ tsp ground ginger
⅔ cup milk
1 lemon
Powdered sugar

Preheat the oven to 325°F. Grease a small bread pan and line it with a strip of waxed paper. Cream together the sugar and butter until light and fluffy.

Gradually beat in the eggs. Sift in the flour and ground ginger. Add enough milk to make a cake batter of thick dropping consistency.

Squeeze the lemon and reserve the juice. Add the rind to the cake mixture and stir in well. Spoon the mixture into the prepared pan and bake about 1 hour in the center of the oven. To test, insert a toothpick or a skewer into the center of the cake; if no batter clings to it, the cake is done.

Lift the cake out of the pan using the strip of waxed paper, and place it on a wire cooling rack.

Mix the reserved lemon juice with enough sifted powdered sugar to make a thin glaze. When the cake is cool, peel off the paper and spoon a layer of the glaze over the top of the cake. Let it dry, then coat again. Let the glaze set completely before slicing the cake.

Sand Tarts

INGREDIENTS
1¼ cups granulated sugar
1 cup butter
1 egg, beaten
2 cups flour
1 egg white, slightly beaten
Sugar
Finely chopped pecans or walnuts

Cream the sugar and butter together until light. Beat in the egg and gradually add the flour, working it in well to make a stiff dough. All the flour may not be necessary.

Chill the mixture overnight, or until firm enough to roll out. Preheat oven to 350°F. Flour a board or pastrycloth well and roll out the dough in small portions. Cut into 2- or 3-inch circles with a cookie cutter.

Place on greased baking sheets. Brush the tops with beaten egg white and sprinkle with a mixture of sugar and nuts. Bake about 10 minutes, or until crisp and pale golden. Leave a few minutes on the baking sheets then remove to wire cooling racks.

Makes 3 dozen

With his dog for company, a boy takes over the reins and practices handling the mule team.

129

Snow Shapes

INGREDIENTS

2 cups butter
3 cups granulated sugar
5 eggs, beaten
1 tsp baking soda, dissolved in ¼ cup boiling
   water
1 cup cream
4 to 5 cups flour
Powdered sugar

Cream the butter and sugar together until light. Beat in the eggs gradually. Stir in the dissolved baking soda and water.

Add the cream, alternating with the flour. Mix thoroughly to form a stiff dough. Knead it lightly and chill about 2 hours.

Preheat the oven to 350°F. Roll out the dough on a well-floured board and use your favorite cookie cutters to cut out shapes. Place cookies on lightly greased baking sheets and bake about 12 minutes, or until very pale, but crisp. Leave on the baking sheets a few seconds, then lift onto wire cooling racks. Dust with sifted powdered sugar.

Although the cattle tower above him, an Amish boy confidently guides the animals back from milking.

Fudge Brownies

INGREDIENTS
2 tbsps butter
1½ squares bitter chocolate
1 tsp vanilla extract
1 cup sugar
2 eggs, beaten
½ cup flour
½ cup chopped walnuts
½ cups semi-sweet chocolate, chopped (or use chocolate chips)
Powdered sugar

Preheat the oven to 350°F. Grease a square, shallow pan. Melt the chocolate and butter in a double boiler or in a bowl over simmering water.

Stir in the vanilla extract and the sugar. Beat in the eggs.

Fold in the flour, then the chopped walnuts and chocolate or chocolate chips. Spoon the mixture into the pan and bake about 20 minutes, or until the top looks dry and the mixture begins to pull away from the sides of the pan. Do not let it overbake or the brownies will be hard and dry.

Cool in the pan, then cut into squares. Dust with powdered sugar, if desired.

*An Amish funeral procession makes its
way through the country lanes.*

Walnut Raisin Cookies

INGREDIENTS
1 cup butter
1½ cups light brown sugar
3 eggs
1 tsp baking soda dissolved in 1½ tbsps hot water
3¼ cups flour
½ tsp salt
1 tsp cinnamon
1 cup walnuts, chopped
1 cup golden raisins

Preheat oven to 350°F. Cream the butter and sugar together until light. Beat in the eggs, one at a time. Add the soda mixture, then work in half of the flour, together with the salt and cinnamon.

Mix in the walnuts and raisins, then the remaining flour. Grease several baking sheets and drop the mixture by spoonfuls about 1 inch apart. Bake about 8 to 10 minutes, or until golden brown.

Makes 3 dozen

Sweet Yeast Biscuits

INGREDIENTS
4 cups milk
4 eggs, beaten
4 tbsps butter, melted
1 yeast cake
½ cup lukewarm water
2 cups sugar
Flour

TOPPING
2 cups sugar
4 tbsps flour
½ cup butter, softened
4 tbsps boiling water

Scald the milk and allow to cool slightly. Beat in the eggs gradually, along with the butter. Cool to lukewarm. Mix the yeast and water and add to the milk mixture with the sugar and enough flour to make a thin batter. Cover and leave in a warm place overnight.

Add enough flour to the mixture to make a soft, pliable dough. Knead it lightly on a well-floured surface. Place in an oiled bowl and leave to rise again until doubled in size.

Knock out the air and knead again lightly. Roll out to an inch thickness and cut out biscuit shapes. Place on an oiled baking sheet and leave to rise again until doubled in size.

Preheat the oven to 400°F. Mix the topping ingredients to a smooth paste and brush over the tops of the biscuits. Bake biscuits about 20 minutes, or until the bottoms sound hollow when tapped.

Makes 1 dozen

A group of Amish children on their way to church. The services are often very long, but the children are well behaved.

Molasses Doughnuts

INGREDIENTS
¾ pint milk
4 cups flour
½ cake of yeast
1½ tbsps molasses
¼ cup butter
1 egg
Oil for deep frying
Sugar

Scald the milk then leave until lukewarm. Stir in half of the flour to make a smooth batter. Dissolve the yeast in a little warm water and add to the batter. Cover and leave to stand at least 8 hours.

Cream the molasses, butter and egg together with a little of the remaining flour. Add to the first mixture. Knead in enough of the remaining flour to make a light dough that can be rolled out. Place in a large greased bowl and cover with a floured cloth. Leave in a warm place to rise until doubled in bulk.

Roll out on a floured board and cut into doughnut rings. Leave to rise again, about 20 minutes.

Heat oil in a deep fryer or pan to about 375°F. Add the doughnuts a few at a time and fry until they rise to the surface and puff up. When they are cooked through, drain them on paper towels. Roll in sugar while still warm, if desired.

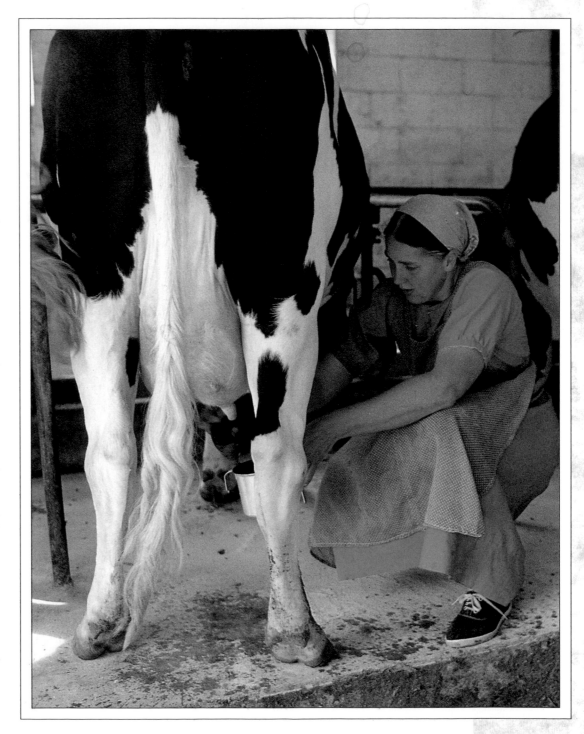

Although some of the Amish still insist on milking by hand, less conservative groups use milking machines.

Streusel Bread

The Amish consider children a gift from God and they are brought up as part of a large, loving family.

INGREDIENTS
½ cup butter
¾ cup sugar
1 cake of yeast
¼ cup lukewarm water
1 cup milk
2 eggs, beaten
2½ to 3 cups bread flour

TOPPING
1¼ cups soft breadcrumbs
1 tsp cinnamon
3 tbsps brown sugar
2 tbsps butter, melted

Cream the butter and the sugar together in a large bowl. Dissolve the yeast in the lukewarm water and leave until frothy.

Scald the milk and add gradually to the butter and sugar. When slightly cooled, add the eggs and the yeast mixture. Mix well, then work in the flour to make a thick batter. Add more flour if the batter is too runny.

Beat the mixture with a spatula or wooden spoon; it will be too soft to knead by hand. Cover the bowl and leave the batter in a cool place to rise until doubled in bulk.

Preheat the oven to 400°F. Grease two deep pie dishes, large loaf pans or brioche pans and spoon in the batter to fill just over halfway.

Mix the topping ingredients together and sprinkle over the top of each bread. Leave in a warm place about 20 minutes to rise again, then bake about 20 minutes, or until golden brown. Serve with butter or jam.

Corn Bread

INGREDIENTS
1 cup yellow cornmeal
1 cup flour
4 tbsps sugar
1 tsp salt
4 tsps baking powder
1 egg, beaten
1 cup milk
2 tbsps shortening, melted

Grease a square baking pan and preheat the oven to 400°F. Mix cornmeal, flour, sugar, salt and baking powder in a large bowl. Make a well in the center and add the egg, milk and melted shortening. Beat very well until the ingredients are thoroughly blended.

Pour batter into the prepared pan and bake until risen and golden brown on top. As a variation, add ¼ cup grated sharp cheese. Cut into squares to serve.

Left: the combined power of horses and mules keeps the corn-picking operation running smoothly.

Index